'A strange and stunning collectio
hilarious and wise, *Seasonal Distu*
ploration of the human condition

Also by Karen McCarthy Woolf
from Carcanet Press

An Aviary of Small Birds
Oxford Poets 2013

SEASONAL DISTURBANCES

Karen McCarthy Woolf

CARCANET

First published in Great Britain in 2017 by
CARCANET PRESS LTD
Alliance House, 30 Cross Street
Manchester M2 7AQ

A CIP catalogue record for this book is available
from the British Library. ISBN 9781784103361

Typeset by XL Publishing Services, Exmouth
Printed & bound in England by SRP Ltd.

The publisher acknowledges financial assistance
from Arts Council England.

Contents

SEASONAL DISTURBANCES

The Hollyhocks

I

The hotel is so luxurious and the black walls
are lit by fleshy-armed candelabras
the flame almost dying in the breeze as she passes
and the horse is restless in the stable,
he hasn't been out for days
and when she sees the text

it's like the parcel of cold sky
hanging over fields covered in snow
and studded with blackened Champagne vines.
Then all of a sudden it's— *when you're together
does she crawl on all fours? What does she drink?
Tell me, I need to know, what does she eat?*

II

She did it for him
even though she shouldn't
have done it; once it was done
she couldn't undo it.

III

O hollyhocks of Ile de Ré
O tunnels of pollen
O wooden boardwalks across the marshes
O pastel petals crushed by bicycle tyres
O seeds planted that won't take
Grow for me again!

IV

The thing about the hollyhocks was to what degree was it about the hollyhocks? Or were they a distraction? That time her ovary pinged like an elastic band as he stood over her in the kitchen insisting on one-inch cubes for the beef.

V

A skeleton leaf tattooed around a scar.

VI

Alcea Rosea, family Malvacaeae. ORIGIN: Middle English: from **holy** + obsolete *hock* 'mallow', of unknown origin. It originally denoted the marsh mallow, which has medicinal uses (hence, perhaps, the use of 'holy');

VII

That which obscures
amplifies the cost.

VIII

In this scenario a detective comes to the house wearing a trenchcoat and a trilby with a feather that looks like a fishing fly tucked into the rim. A woman lets him in and offers him a drink. He asks for a glass of water. When she leaves the room the detective takes a pack of Camel from his coat pocket and offers one to the husband who is sitting on the sofa. The husband declines and clears his throat and the man tells him he's here on account of the hollyhocks.

The detective gets out a little flip notebook and a retracting pencil. The woman says the husband wouldn't leave it alone, even when they stood by the French window, his arm looped around her waist, his head bent to her neck. He still pressed her to take action.

There must have been about thirty altogether as she piled them on to a pyre-like mound.

In retrospect she felt this unprovoked attack on their fecundity was a bad omen and one which was made manifest later down the line. The husband interjects at this point to say she has it all wrong. *It was only a suggestion.*

The detective makes a note of this in his notebook, snaps it shut and returns the retracting pencil to his top pocket. Then he stands up, shakes hands with the couple, swigs the rest of the melted ice from his glass and leaves.

Conversation, with Water

Lying on the floor of the wheelhouse sensitises the body
to movement and sound:
the thrum of the generator on its last legs, a swoosh of fuel in the tank.

Hence*

As the wind blows
            innumerable plump and hideous
landfolk
insignificant in themselves but rich—

            It is a strange world

no birds nesting or singing in the trees;
no bellowing, roaring or squeaking savage or small;
no caterpillars to eat the leaves; no bees
or butterflies; no creatures that do more than crawl.

* An Ode

                        Another
spasm   was being prepared
                and the climate
began   to change.

Up on the Hill

A young Bulgarian who comes
to clear the old mattress and carpet
out of the bedroom
            asks if Spring
always arrives so early here?
The forsythia's not out yet
so things must be as they should be.
            There's an order
to the colours: snowdrop,
daffodil yellow, forget me not,
followed by brash sunset dahlia.
            Up on the Hill
by the edge of Rush Common where
tree-fall debris mingles
with bottle tops, a pair of discarded socks
            and crows
poke at the mud, the wrens
are nocturnal now, in order that
their song might be heard over
            the babble of traffic
rumbling up the hill like a brook
inexplicably flowing backwards;
they sing, these birds
            up above the smoke
you can only see from a distance, brown
and insistent as a river,
            on nights
when we walk, lips purple
with wine, past the 24-hour shop,
arguing about who said what and
            nothing that matters.

On the Thames

The houseboat tilts into the water at low tide,
ducklings slip in mud. Nothing is stable
in this limbo summer, where he leaves
his shoes in the flat— She decides to let
a room, the ad says only ten minutes to the tube,
I have a washing machine and a cat. The truth
more of a struggle than anyone cares to admit.
And everywhere progress: an imprint of cranes
on the skyline, white vans on bridges, the Shard
shooting up to the light like a foxglove.

Most birds travel in pairs.
Or at least here, one notices most birds when they travel in pairs,
    skimming close to the surface over water that flutters—

It feels good up on the freshly painted deck.

—all this time from my vantage point I've looked left to the Commons
and the Lords, not towards St Thomas's,
with its walled garden where I sat cradling ghosts, the pain
so white and intermingled.

Gulls

Returning to Arrecife after
half a lifetime I notice how
there are no
gulls at the Marina
and wonder
where or if they are now—
Is this the last, on the prow
of a glistening schooner?

Inland, at the vast
malodorous tip
thousands wheel above red
earth, wings cast
to the putrid scraps
on which they must feed.

The pull of the tide is how certain women are drawn in and get dragged under.

Abyss

—until recently, only females
were known. Eventually
some of these females were discovered
to have growing on their bodies
strange objects not unlike
miniature and deformed fish.

Further investigation
showed these to be the long looked-for
male of the species. When quite young
they apparently bite on the female,
gradually embedding their snout.

Both skin and blood-vessels
of male and female grow together, and the male
becomes a true parasite, nourished entirely
at the female's expense.

To Dover from Calais

After midnight we drive through Sangatte
on the outskirts, where teenagers rush to the tunnel.

In the big-cat gleam of our headlamps
the boys pause for a heartbeat— disappear in a flash.

If you're not really a Syrian
is it safer in the Congo, or Afghanistan?

While we all fiddle with our smartphones
sniffer dogs inhale the articulated lorry.

Two ferrymen tell me how they feel
okay because they pull up the bridge and sail away.

It's only a joke if it's funny
so I don't laugh at 'they weren't exactly *invited*'.

Soldiers career up and down the river on manoeuvres. Children in canoes capsize in their wake.

I open *The Pillow Book* on p. 23 to [22] *list of dispiriting things:*
a dog howling in the middle of the day. The sight in spring of a trap for
catching winter fish. Robes in the plum/pink combination when it's now the
third or fourth month...

The pull of the tide is the pull of the moon.

an oxkeeper whose ox has died. A birthing hut where the baby has died.

Kingfisher

The truth is I've a long history of dead birds
        and there's been no cadavers since
those first months mourning my baby son, so

when I find her, at the top of some steps
        on a ledge leading to a beach, full of tourists
sheltering from the heat under striped *ombrelloni*,

I do what I always do and lean in to take a picture.
        I have no idea this fallen star is Halcyon,
immortal daughter of Aeolus, keeper of the winds

and namesake of the Islands shimmering
        on the horizon— A turquoise streak
over mottled green suggests a juvenile. I wonder

        why she's here, on a beach, rather than by the river.
Empty eye sockets contradict an immaculate plumage:
        she's out of place. At least that's what I think.

In truth this is Halcyon's homeland, her story ends
        and begins on this iridescent strip
of waves that become her widow's pyre and grave.

The Gods were kinder than expected and resurrect
        Ceyx and his grief-struck wife,
turn them into birds (kingfishers to be exact)

        but as is the way with these things, there's a catch.
Halcyon must lay her eggs in winter
        and when she returns to nest at the water's edge

the chicks are always swept offshore.
        Naturally, her sorrow is immense
and she wails and begs until Aeolus is permitted

        to hold the winds at bay over the winter solstice,
so the storms are calmed and the fledglings prevail.
        Now, even in summer, the crowded boats capsize

and there are no patriarchs with open arms
        who protect the young and control weather.
There are no Halcyon Days; the sea itself is dying.

Blot out all my iniquities. Create in me a clean heart.

It makes me think of the cat, how he likes to lick drops from the tap.
I am a small girl who forgets to wash her hands.

I have a life jacket and am prepared to swim.

It's true, there's a lot of weather here and I also saw a bird with a neck bent
like a crowbar perched on top of an industrial winch, scanning for eels.

Christmas Eve

When the tree falls in the storm
                    three garages are destroyed
and you are not mine anymore

                    asbestos swirls in the air
this flat, full only of things
                    a detritus of branches, cars

Variation (Untitled)

could one ginger cat really be so different
to another ginger cat? one tall, the other also (if less)
inconstant, both with belly swinging, white chest flash—
who wants the next one

to be like the last? also there are
subtle yet overt differences, such as
in America where the kitchens are unexpectedly old-fashioned
with top-loading washing machines
and you thought everything would be equal
because everyone speaks English /   but

        the reality is one cat was replaced by another
after an implausibly brief pause
which made the whole thing seem glossy
like a svelte coat on a domestic shorthair or a lie

O River, here I am, riding on your back in a little dinghy they call a rib.
It's like clinging to a grizzly by the scruff of the neck.

Who knows what the water might shake out of me.

I confess   must be nautical in origin.

Ars Poetica 101

Golden Shovel after Elizabeth Alexander

Poetry
John says, lays claims on the heart (and
also the head), that now
he reads it with more personal attention; my
feeling is the voice
as a conduit for love is
necessary as blood (is diligent as sap rising)

Poetry is
how we accept what we're not
—is all sticky-green-tender and choral, all
we, you or I have, love
being so seemingly— love
being the verb we must wait for in a subordinate clause, love
as a synonym for silly and

O, how I wish I wasn't sorry
for not replying to your letter with the
pressed snowdrop, that arrived, faithful as a dog
who returns, doggedly, to the spot where his mistress died.

Poetry
is testy as friendship (here
I confess I
tend to hear
you as a muffled version of myself
and if not wise, I'm loudest)

Poetry is
what the sea sings to the
last insatiable human
who thinks he's the only one with a voice

to flood the dark with music and
dance or wonder who we are
and why we're here or how we
became I, so exclusively— not
that the long-lashed ox knows any more of
cathedral spires, his interest
is in trees and grass, he doesn't care to
reach beyond low-hanging fruit. Why, when each
exquisite blade tastes just like the other?

Holes and corners

The males scurry over the surface
and pop sideways in and out
of the holes
and reproduce themselves
by making dibbles
and in the course of six to eight months
develop a long, solid spike-like
outgrowth, a foot or eighteen inches
long and up to an inch or more
thick, which forces its way.
At last the whole embryo,
now weighing about three ounces,
breaks loose from its parent, and falls,
heavy and spear-like.

Although it's obvious, the experience is all about staying in the same place while strong currents rush to their destination.

River, I sense part of your job is to take our emotional detritus and wash it out to sea.

Poem in Which I'm Pleased to Have Opted

for the mechanical scales, rejecting the digital set
with lithium battery: they are made in China and cost
five pounds and this weighs on me like a pair of earrings
tugging at the hole. What if I were as efficient as the hollyhocks
that suck all life out of the crack in my concrete terrace,
their tips nudging at the windowsill of the woman upstairs?
My heart is numb as a lobe frozen for piercing, hardly an ideal
condition, but I persevere and note the most beautiful thing
I have seen by four p.m. is the half-Chinese (half-what?)
woman with the cinched waist in the sports department
who was worried when I told her I'd weighed myself
twice a day since I was fourteen. *I live for the ecstasy
of food* I added by way of reassurance, my heart beating
a little faster after the second double espresso that morning.

& Because

a string of unilluminated dragonflies dangles
from the ceiling

our screens glow
like fireflies
at opposite ends of the flat, one of us
facing south, the other
north,

the anglepoise reflected
like a moon in the cracked glass— yes,
it's cracked but it endures,
the empty spaces I crave are filled
with dust
dating back to the nineteenth century

& because I can't forget
the torrent
of the M6 as we switched
lanes on the way back from the retrospective
where we took
photos of you standing by a painting
of your mother in 1975,
how she stared
out of a window, determined
not to smile
and of course your hair is the colour of her hair,
and the gallery walls are white

& because roses aren't what they used to be, so few
are fragrant and only a fraction
of those that survive the shivery hold
unfurl into fullness,
their thorns
bred out like pips from a watermelon

&
because water is no longer sacred, our rivers
run like sores
and mountain streams are bottled, sold,
binned then spun
into the gyres of the Pacific

Prone

In big cities
there has been a great deal of independent
losing.

The old and simple types continue
but it is
shot through with progress.

On the whole animals
analyse purely
— it is best to leave values out.

If a tapeworm
could for a moment be granted the power
he would confess

that his was a blind alley
apparently without limit.

Happiness

when one locust meets another
the nervous system releases
serotonin, causing a mutual attraction
(a prerequisite for swarming)

(a prerequisite for swarming)
serotonin, causing a mutual attraction
the nervous system releases
when one locust meets another

The Sin

It grows a fishing rod and bait on its head
It is elongated, detached—

Numerous members of this same family
attract their prey by means of lures,
always luminous.
The prowling population can never be
without special advertisement.

Sometimes there is a single row of small
lights down the body; sometimes
tiers of lights, like a liner at night.
Its own identity
written upon it in letters of cold fire.

The benefit conferred in return is normally
protection.

Jay tells me living on water is hard and expensive.

I decide to conduct an experiment. I will find water. I open Haruki Murakami's *What I Talk About When I Talk About Running* on page 90: 'Seeing a lot of water every day is probably an important thing for human beings. *For human beings* might be a bit of a generalisation – but I do know it's important for one person: me. If I go for a long time without seeing water, I feel like something's slowly draining out of me.'

Number 19

The back door has a glass pane, obscured
by a mediaeval dragon with Hebrew tattooed on its belly.

Outside the French windows an ebony monkey
crouches over a circumcision bowl designed to catch blood.

The front door is purple with a metal grille
over reinforced glass and is kept double locked.

Even a frayed rope can tether a boat.

Tatler's People Who Really Matter

Although you might think them wildly intimidating,
many are astonishingly cosy and nice.

She is not a perfect English Rose,
but he has the loveliest, gorgeous glossy hair.

Imagine how super-clever and super-connected
and affable one must be to have got this far.

Considering they are not all trained, many
are relentlessly upbeat and frighteningly talented.

Boundlessly energetic, they approach each border
as if it were new, even after umpteen impressive attempts.

Mind-blowingly otter-faced, she tells the little ones
everything's going to be just fine— the lie

flawless as pale skin, some might call it pneumatic.
When they get through it is delightful.

The closest is lying with my head in my mother's lap,
                         the thickness of the paint, bottle green and grey—

In reality I give thanks for the barrier, your reinforced banks.
There's something in *spreading yourself thin*.

Day of the Dead

She's shut you in
her trophy box.

There is no key.
It has no lock.

You climbed inside
with throbbing cock.

Now hope that someone
hears you knock.

Yesterday, at the make-up counter the girl who was colour-matching my foundation said that men are attracted to moisture: it is scientifically proven. The answer was lip gloss but now I realise this is why I think of you, Dear River, as female, as feminine: all water is, I am beginning to believe that.

Horse Chestnut I — A Coupling

from a letter from DARWIN, C.R. *to* HOOKER, J.D., *22 May 1860*

P.S. | As Horse-chestnuts have male flowers
when a man comes into his flowering season

& hermaphrodite flowers I have wished to examine
with petals soft and tender as breasts, open to bare

their pollen,
his seed

& this has made me observe
& this has made me

a thing which has surprised me.— All the flowers
an entreaty, flowering labiatae

now open on my *several* trees
now open and in profusion

are *male* with rudimentary pistil
are female too, rude and raw

with *pollen shedding*; so that I began to think
how dishevelled I was, how

my memory had deceived me
into enamour

& that the pistil was never well developed;
& that the pestle was a well, deep and enveloped

but on opening
as I opened, my eyes like

buds near the end of each little lateral twig
sticky, overt, receptive

of the flower-truss, I find
a cluster &

plenty of hermaphrodite flowers with pistils
in abundance, asphodels forever pulsing, pert yet

well developed. So that on all my trees
these trees, my roots, these roots attest

there has been a gigantic crop of *quite useless*
ideas. & O, how intoxicating the air, as

male flowers, with millions of pollen-grains wasted,
open, as the male, he flowers, swollen and unsated

for there is not a female flower nearly open.—
For there is not a female or a flower so open.

Evolution

A man is really very like a frog;
brain in a brain box; eyes, ears, nose,
mouth and teeth but unlike
the vast man-frog plan
man is more like a frog than a fish
for frog and man possess
and a fish does not
but man is less like a frog than a dog,
for man and dog both have hair and divided hearts
and warm blood of several different sorts
and milk
and frogs have none of these things

In terms of classification men and dogs are
frogs are not

Of Ownership

Golden Shovel after Joy Harjo

The verb has a long history of violence: to take
is to grab, seize or capture, esp. by force; note
its hard 'k' set against the long vowel, a sign of
intent, this cave of sound. *He took her by the
throat and shook her* is one in a proliferation
of examples. To enter into possession or use of
(a thing) any thing, the things of supermarkets
that lull us as we push the trolley round and
round the soothing fountains in the malls,
always the polystyrene trays of flesh bright in the
fluorescent aisle. Our virgins at such altars
now are birds who've never felt the drum of
rain on their fattened breasts. Save money.
Buy one, get one free & variations thereon. They
(the shops) are here to help themselves as best
they can. Language is also ownership, we describe
our thoughts, and by default corral the
heart: most articulation is squandered as a detour
from love that manifests as pain inside us, from
what is felt, from breath that connects us to grace.

True Love

We learn to conjugate *être*
before *avoir*; a mystery made overt
by absence, this unstrung lute—

Imagine a tree,
an abundant avocado, the lure
of creamy fruit: revel
in it, allow your eyes to rove
the room for ever.

        When it's over
pain scratches a route
to the heart, quick as an elver
and on repeat: a brutal lout.

The act no man can veto.
Bow to its rule.

There are many thicknesses of rope.
Or, woodsmoke drifts from the chimney like breath. A knife in its sheaf on the window ledge.

Argument

On this day of sharp and localised pain
I think of you as a disagreeable cloud that won't
stop raining, or rather one that rains just after
I've watered the geraniums, or
you're a cloud that hovers and won't
rain when the garden needs it, blocking
all things cerulean, and although I say I'm useless
at standoffs, the truth is I know how to incubate
silence if I have to, so now, seeing
as neither of us is willing to concede even
a missed call, I'm forced to take comfort in
an artificial sunset projected onto Southwark Bridge
and the churn of river from the back of the boat
that flows like blood between sisters.

Verbs I Have Seen in Relation to Migrants, With Cranes

North, south and east, they congregate, a conglomerate.
Sky Crane, Crawler Crane, Sidelifter, Fixed—

Rough Terrain Crane is good for nothing but throwing rocks,
Tower Crane hovers, hurls, occasionally prevaricates.

Pitted against the horizon, their shadows unleashed
on the river's surface— glassy as Canary Wharf's pyramid.

Erect in salute, red and white arms rigid,
they push on, into newly smuggled, allocated space.

Here

They come because this is the future
and there's money to be made, because being
here is better than there, where they were,
before they were here. They move in
next door and across the road. They open
shops selling unfamiliar things many
of us are yet to taste. New people work
in the new shops. New customers come to take
pictures, speaking in strange tongues.

At first there were just a few of them, now
they're everywhere you look. They all
drink boutique coffee out of jam jars, they all
buy up old houses close to the park.

Some assimilate; Others do not.

Conquest

—the word itself has a nasty
                crawling
and to that has been added

            a mythical cold
sliminess, partly from forgetfulness
but mainly from the fact

that the lie and its most remarkable products
must be continually lubricated
and kept moist.

You have only to watch
to see a creature which has retained
for three hundred million years

this primitive method
of support and progression.

A review of Masaru Emoto's book about the shapes water crystals make when you say the words *love* and *gratitude* says *Emoto frequently appeals to coincidence as significant, then jumps to puzzling conclusions unsupported by his chain of events.*

Voyage

of the Damned
is a film from the 1970s
starring Faye Dunaway with her cat's eyes
and cheekbones

Irpinia
is the name of the ship
the producers chartered
to use as the set

Many Rivers to Cross
was your favourite song
as requested we played it
at your funeral

Irpinia
is the name of the ship
you board at Kingston Harbour
where you had 'a good job'
as a customs official

Voyage of the Damned
is a film set on a ship in 1939
when a thousand Jewish refugees
fled Germany for Cuba

Irpinia
is a region south of Naples
full of mountains and many rivers
its name means wolf
in the language of the ancient tribes

Voyage of the Damned
is a true story
where the wolf wears a uniform
and spits out bones and teeth

Dunns River
is a brand of ackee
a fruit that's poisonous if picked unripe
it only comes here tinned

On the Irpinia
you organise a committee
of West Indian chefs
to cook for those who find the food too 'fresh'
a term that doesn't mean the same thing
as it does in England

Rivers of …
is misquoted
and comes from the legend of Aeneas
who said he saw the Tiber
course through his city of wolves
foaming with much blood

Irpinia
is close to the hot mouth of Vesuvius
a verdant passage from
the Tyrrhenian to the Adriatic

Voyage of the Damned
was transatlantic
the liner set sail for the Caribbean
full of hope
and families looking for a way in

Cassava River
runs in-between Above Rocks
and Glengoffe
the village from which your mother Katharine Weir
migrated to the capital

On the Irpinia
people are crowded into dorms
like cattle stalls
in the middle of the ocean

Voyage of the Damned
is a tale of propaganda and dodgy visas
The Nazis knew
Cuba never planned to take the refugees
even as a stepping stone

Irpinia's
passenger log
has your date of birth wrong
it's hardly a luxury liner
the Grimaldi brothers snapped the fleet up cheap
seeing promise in the migrant market

Golden River
froths downstream
from Mizpah, Zion Hill and Sooky Gal
in your childhood parish

Irpinia's
earthquake of the 1980s
left three hundred thousand homeless

Voyage of the Damned
was doomed
SS St Louis sailed back to Europe
where countries quibbled over quotas
only a third
made it through the War alive

The Irpinia
docks at Southampton
you're here
to join your sons and wife
a nurse called Cutie, in a fledgling NHS
hungry for a beginning

On the sixth day of the fifth month when the moon is godknowswhere:
a pair of Canada geese and four goslings nudge
at stones to dislodge worms in the mud at low tide,
the chicks orbiting the mother.

The river swallows time as a whale swallows plankton,
although plankton, we now know, is no longer a certainty.

Seasonal Disturbances

On the night of the hurricane
I slept right through it, then got up
while it was still dark and went to work,
wondering why the streets were empty
and there were no cars on the road.
The wind was ovenish and I made it
to Paddington. All the connections
were running when others were cancelled
and I knew something wasn't right.
It was blowy, the air was unseasonably
warm and I hated how I was wasting my
youth, even then, when I was in it. I knew
this path was wrong, but I kept on
fluttering down it, like a piece of paper
that was creased but blank. My train
was the only train running, so
I got on, made my way in to the office
where everyone else was white
and the two typesetters I managed always
queried my edits and all along the way looking
out of the window from the empty carriage
I could see trees blown over,
their roots curling up into the air.

Staring at the surface does not provide answers
to philosophical or practical questions: for a grebe however,
this activity can yield eels.

[And is it wrong to say something about wanting to kill
myself?]

Every new construction

leaves a demolition in its wake
and cranes cluster round the towers, crowding
the water's edge. Here, anchorage is sold
by the square metre and the Queen still owns the river bed.

This is the final enclosure.

The sun shines hard as the spokes of the Eye and it's the warmest
July since records began. I try to buy an iced soya latte
on the River Bus, but the girl says *no*, so I order a cappuccino
with cow's milk instead and ask for a cup filled with ice cubes only
I'm not quick enough to reject the moulded white lid
which now she'll chuck and I blame her for in my head
until I remember— I said *yes* without thinking to the plastic
straw with ridges that bend— as I take my seat by the window
looking out at the pier where the empty Hilton ferry docks.

A Death

speeded up in the mind's eye
a paroxysm spread

Europe heaved in sympathy
worn down to such stumps

what caused it is not
our business

its onset due to
central heating

      this infected all sea
      and filled it full of accumulating
      bits of India and possibly Central Africa
      right up to the equator. The Northern Hemisphere
      was no escape as the earth grew a new plan
      to meet the new conditions— smaller and less luxuriant.

According to Mr Emoto water does not like listening to heavy metal. Also, did he change his name to Emoto to echo emotion?

Outside

under the arcade
and the floor-length glass shop front:
a green pop-up dome

flanked by a Burberry
suitcase and a sleeping bag

a makeshift shelter
for Sai from Stratford
with time to invest

in a four-day queue— he's first
in line for an iPhone 6s

no-one moves him on
or threatens arrest
as it's not about where

but why you pitch your tent

But the heart is not in service to the mind, as a scullery maid on her knees, brushing and brushing while Victorian gentlemen gape at her red knuckles swollen with work.

The CEO

When barbed wire fences
were first introduced
there were many cases
of the new-fangled fences
learning directly from the old.

May it not be
that they owe their fleshiness
to the cumulative effect?

Perhaps, but not necessarily.

Some very fair people
burn and suffer. It is so essential
any further mutations
towards skin were seized.
This is in itself just.

The Neighbourhood

An estate agent window shatters
any hope of securing cheap accommodation.

Who gave you keys to this city, Mayor?
How did we all forget your plan needs our permission?

Yesterday our grocers closed their doors
because they can't afford to sell olives anymore.

If I don't stop talking politics
I'll have no old friends to sit down and eat cake with.

They sold Ethiopian coffee.
They've gone and now we sell Ethiopian coffee.

Do you remember that architect?
He told us straight: *not everyone gets to have a view.*

In her dream she's still a resident.
When she wakes up she's got no money to pay the rent

They tell me the bridge-jumpers fight, find out they want
to live in the end.

A boat has its own life cycle and itinerary:
driftwood must be collected, dried, chopped
at least two weeks in advance
or the fire will go out.

Her Anger

It takes two to make a meal— the
eaten and the eater—

and the world
can weigh on the system like a dirty cloth,
hastily chewed

delicate machinery can be upset
or a septic focus can poison it.

If only it was as simple as that!

The following simple experiment
is instructive—

Fill the mouth with smoke; put the lips
into the kissing position; hold a reasonably clean
handkerchief taut across them;
eject.

The experiment is pleasing. It also makes me think Murakami is like that. When I was reading *The Wind-Up Bird Chronicle* I got on to the tube carriage, sat down and settled in to my book. The man opposite was reading. It was the same book. We looked up at each other and recognised the swimming pool-blue jacket. I think he was slightly ahead of me.

Landay

Darling, your affair was obvious.
Only an imbecile could have been oblivious.

Now, at the back of my mind there's an inkling that since I decided on the zuihitsu everyone in the poem is suddenly Japanese. And that Japan is also an island, a cluster of islands. Does it then follow that the shapes wind makes in sand dunes reassure the inhabitants?

The Island

Underwater, sun flickers like
a conversation we're yet to have, bright

as the polystyrene cup bobbing
on the surface with the yachts.

Everything resembles something else
when light refracts: translucent

medusas turn into puffball plastic bags
as I soar through the blue

gazing down on schools of little fish.
You say the moon touches the sea

like a stone when you skim it. A stone
is a ball of carbon mozzarella over lunch.

In lieu of the volcano a row flares up.
Obsidian glitters against white walls.

Horse Chestnut II — A Coupling

from MATSUO BASHŌ, *The Narrow Road to the Deep North*

'There was a huge chestnut tree
once there was a large horse chestnut

on the outskirts of this post town,
on the border of my home

and a priest walking in seclusion
always when I was alone and sometimes

under its shade. When I stood here
looking up into the light

in front of the tree, I felt as if I were
a viridescent umbrella, I felt as if I were

in the midst of the deep mountains
in the arms of a man, my love, who lived

where the poet Saigyo had picked nuts,
to please me.

I took a piece of paper from
I tore a piece of paper from

my bag, and wrote as follows:
my book

'The chestnut is a holy tree,
'A holy tree is the chestnut

for the Chinese ideograph for chestnut,
its seed scattered and brown

is Tree placed directly below West,
is all one could ever hope for in

the direction of the Holy Land.
A tree reaching up to the sun!

The priest Gyoki is said to have used it
—every day, as I gazed into its canopy,

for his walking stick
for protection

and the chief support of his house.'
My support.

O River I submit to your rhythmic dictatorship and propensity for ruthless, expansionist acts.

You are the centre of our forgetfulness...

And the wind does not blow in the right direction all the time, and sometimes not at all, or too hard.

—all we had for company were lilies of the valley—

words stream past me
                    disturbed surfaces   reflecting clouds

Rain slashes the window like claws.

Notes

1. 'Conversation, with Water' begins on page 10 and runs throughout the book with the first line in italics. It is a disrupted zuihitsu , a prose-poetry form that developed from Sei Shōnagon's *Pillow Book* and was recently popularised by Kimiko Hahn. Written on board 'November', a Dutch barge on the Thames, it was commissioned for broadcast, with soundscape by BBC Radio 3.

2. *The Science of Life* found-sonnet sequence is taken from the encyclopaedia of the same name by H.G. Wells, Julian Huxley and G.P. Wells (Cassell, 1931). It was written in response to eXXpedition, a transatlantic all-women's sailing mission investigating the impact of micro-plastic pollution on marine and human life, which the author supported as an associate artist in 2014. The numbers within the poem titles correspond to page numbers from the volume.

3. The collection contains two 'couplings': an interventionist, hybrid form, devised by the author, where a passage of pre-existing prose is lineated and a response line that includes assonance, repetition or rhyme is written underneath to create a new lyric narrative. For more on the form see *Mslexia* 64 or *www.mccarthywoolf.com*. 'Horse Chestnut II – A Coupling' uses an excerpt from *The Narrow Road to the Deep North and Other Travel Sketches*, Matsuo Bashō, translated by Noboyuki Yuasa (Penguin, 1966).

4. 'Ars Poetica 101' and 'Of Ownership' are 'golden shovels', a derivative form invented by Terrance Hayes in celebration of Gwendolyn Brooks, in which a line from one poem provides the end words for a new piece. 'Ars Poetica 101' is from Elizabeth Alexander's 'Ars Poetica 100'; 'Of Ownership' is from Joy Harjo's 'A Map to the Next World'. For more see *www.poetryfoundation.org*. 'True Love' hybridises a sonnet with a 'Gram of &', an anagrammatic form also devised by Hayes.

5. '*Tatler*'s People Who Really Matter' takes its title, adverbs and adjectives from the magazine's 'rich list' of the same name.

Acknowledgements

Thanks are due to the editors of the following journals and magazines in which some of these poems were first published: *Enchanting Verses, Magma, Mslexia, Ploughshares, The Poetry Review, The Rialto,* and *The Scores.* Thanks also to Malika Booker and Miriam Nash; Paula Bader; Jo Shapcott and Robert Hampson at Royal Holloway; Mimi Khalvati and the 'Tuesday group'; Nathalie Teitler and Bernardine Evaristo at The Complete Works; Susan Roberts at BBC Radio 3 for commissioning 'Conversation, with Water'; Judith Chernaik at Poems on the Underground for selecting 'On the Thames'; Lucy and Jay at The November Project; Lucy Gilliam and Emily Penn at eXXpedition/Pangea Exploration; Sophie Herxheimer and Joanna Salter at the National Maritime Museum for their work with me on *Voyage*; Rocío Ceron and The British Council, Mexico City for commissioning 'True Love' and 'Every new construction' as part of Transmedia Shakespeare 2016.